Carnival
in Rio

For Karin and Christine

HELMUT TEISSL

Carnival
in Rio

ABBEVILLE PRESS PUBLISHERS New York London Paris

É carnaval!

RIO'S EXUBERANCE
AND SENSUALITY

*C*arnival is all the little festivals and parades in the streets and *favelas,* Rio de Janeiro's poor quarters. Carnival is also masked balls, elegant and often uninhibited— even debauched, where one sees fewer masks but plenty of skin. And Carnival is a time for competitions in which countless participants pay thousands of dollars for luxurious and fantastic costumes.

But Carnival is also a time of fraternization, tolerance, and genuine human fellowship.

Rio's Carnival has become internationally famous largely for the grand *desfile,* or review, of the top samba schools, the most colorful carnival procession in the world.

At Carnival, Rio's clocks start running on a different time.

The roots of Rio's Carnival can be found in the eighteenth-century Portuguese entertainment called the *entrudo.* In that festival, celebrants pelted each other with small containers of water, perfume, and sometimes even foul-smelling liquids. The first masked balls were held in 1835, and the first rhythm band, Ze Pereira, beat its drums through the streets of Rio in 1852. That sound continues to be the musical foundation for Carnival. The first carnival society was founded in 1855, and others soon followed. Because decorated floats became part of the parades then, Rio's Carnival as we know it dates back to 1855.

The Banda da Carmen Miranda

A GAUDY BUT SMALLER PARADE

A few days before the grand parade itself, the Banda da Carmen Miranda stages its own procession in the Ipanema district. The *banda* is a somewhat loosely organized group that adopted the name of the famous samba singer of the 1940s for its lavish style of costumes. For all its outlandish get-ups (and the resulting hopeless traffic jams!), this parade cannot begin to compare in size with the processions of the samba schools. Nevertheless, it is noted for its tremendous creativity and sense of fun.

Pagode

MUSIC FOR THE SOUL

*P*agode are the popular folk festivals where the samba originated, and they are especially well attended at Carnival time. It is here that the *cariocas,* or inhabitants of Rio, hone their musical skills.

The atmosphere is extremely casual, and listeners join in singing songs about their troubles and aspirations (CD track **1**). Rotating musicians often play without a break until dawn, as though to demonstrate that a true love of life leaves no time for sleep.

Escolas de Samba

CARNIVAL YEAR-ROUND

*T*he *escolas de samba,* or samba schools, are by no means academies in the traditional sense. They are carnival societies, much like the crewes of New Orleans' Mardi Gras festival. The name "school" derives from the fact that the first of the carnival societies, Deixa Falar ("Let Them Talk"), happened to meet—illegally at that time—in the Estácio district across the street from an elementary school. The next societies to be established were Mangueira and Portela, both in the 1920s. Today there are 60 *escolas de samba* in Rio. They are a major social force and a distinctly positive one, fostering a sense of community and belonging. For many in the *favelas,* they serve as extended families and provide needed assistance. Some of them, like Mangueira, maintain their own health clinics.

The annual carnival parades cost the samba schools enormous amounts of money. They raise much of it from ticket sales, television broadcasting rights, and dance events. Additional funds come in the form of gifts from members and sponsorships from the business community—and it is an open secret that some of the money comes from illegal gambling.

The samba schools are subject to a strict hierarchy. The highest rank, with 14 *escolas de samba,* is the so-called Grupo Especial. Next comes Grupo A, made up of ten samba schools. Both of these groups compete in the grand parade on the Rua Marquês de Sapucaí. Groups B, C, and D, with 12 samba schools each, parade on other streets, notably the Avenida Rio Branco.

Each samba school has its own distinct traditional colors, which are incorporated into their costumes and floats.

	Founded	Traditional colors
PORTELA	1923	blue and white
Estação Primeira de MANGUEIRA	1928	green and pink
Unidos de VILA ISABEL	1946	blue and white
Unidos de VIRADOURO	1946	red and white
Império SERRANO	1947	green and white
BEJA FLOR de Nilopolis	1948	blue and white
CAPRICHOSOS de Pilares	1949	blue and white
União da ILHA do Governador	1953	red, white, and blue
Acadêmicos do SALGUEIRO	1953	red and white
MOCIDADE Independente de Padre Miguel	1955	green and white
IMPERATRIZ Leopoldinense	1959	white and green
SÃO CLEMENTE	1961	black and yellow
TRADIÇÃO	1984	blue and white
Acadêmicos do GRANDE RIO	1988	green, white, and red

Carnavalescos

THE DESIGNERS

Compositores

MUSIC IN THEIR BLOOD

The designers of the parades, called *carnavalescos,* are highly sought artists. For them Carnival is a career. Within weeks of the end of one year's Carnival they start developing the theme *(enredo)* for the next one. They are responsible for their school's costumes, floats, and choreography. It is their concept that determines the school's success or failure in the grand parade.

Joãosinho Trinta (above) is one of the most successful *carnavalescos*. He is determined to astonish with his ideas, and a school with him in charge has a good chance of winning the title. He won for Beja Flor three years in a row in 1976–78, and in 1997 Viradouro won its first victory under his direction.

The rhythm of the samba is like a heartbeat to the *compositores* (composers) of the various schools. In a city like Rio de Janeiro, where music is such an important aspect of people's lives, they enjoy the highest respect. For each Carnival they compose several possible songs for their given school. The best are then selected in a school competition. Their lyrics must relate to the school's chosen theme, or points are deducted by the judges.

Puxadores

THE VOICES OF THE SAMBA

For more than three decades, Jamelão (above) has been presenting the songs of the samba school Mangueira with his powerful voice (CD tracks **5, 7, 8, 13, 17, 18**). The 80 minutes of a parade present an extreme challenge for singers. The *puxador,* or lead singer, is supported by other voices and the huge amplification system of the Sambódromo, or samba stadium, but even so, his performance is the ultimate test of even for the most professional singers.

Bateria

THE DRIVING FORCE

The *bateria,* the samba school's rhythm section, is made up of as many as 350 men.

With its archaic sound, like that of a speeding steam locomotive (CD track **9**, 2:10–3:00), it is the force that drives the entire "train." More than a half mile long, it is the beating heart of the entire *escola.*

At the start of the parade, the *bateria* takes up its position at the entrance to the Sambódromo, playing at full volume and cheered on by the spectators (CD track **2**). Later, it moves into roughly the center of the march. After two-thirds of the parade has passed, the *bateria* pulls out and continues to play on the side.

The dancers of the second half of the samba school now pass the rhythm section, by now in full swing. After this climax, the *bateria* falls in behind the school and follows it to the Praça da Apoteose, where it disperses.

Each samba school has its own instrumentation and playing style, characterized by its *viradas,* or rhythmic changes, and *paradinhas,* or pauses.

At the difficult *paradinhas* programmed by the *bateria* of the Mocidade Independente de Padre Miguel in the 1970s (CD track **14**), all the musicians suddenly stopped playing, leaving the song to be continued by the voices of the singers and dancers alone (CD track **16**, 0:27–0:36). After the pause, the *bateria* rejoins them, to the delight of both dancers and spectators (CD track **2**, 4:10–4:18).

Instruments

THE RHYTHMIC DOZEN

The number of its various instruments determines the *bateria's* unique sound.

The *escola* Império Serrano, for example, is known for the metallic clang of its many *agogôs,* or cowbells, struck with wooden sticks (CD track **6**), which other *baterias* do not use at all. Ilha do Governador achieves its own characteristic sound from the many *caixas,* or snare drums, played with sticks in both hands (CD tracks **2** and **20**). And the Mocidade *bateria* gets its bright, rattling quality from its predominance of tambourines, *cuicas,* and *chocalhos* (CD track **14**).

In a brief solo, the *repique* or *repinique,* a drum played with only one stick and the flat of the hand, heralds the entrance of the entire *bateria* (CD track **14**, 1:00–1:25).

The bass is provided by three *surdos* of different sizes. The largest, the *surdo de marcação,* alternates with the *surdo resposta,* or "answerer" (CD track **9**, 7:30–8:15), while the *surdo cortador* adds in-between beats and syncopation (CD track **9**, 8:16–8:34).

The Mangueira, appearing in its traditional colors of pink

and green, only uses the largest *surdo,* stressing the second beat in each measure. This produces the school's characteristic stumbling rhythm (CD tracks **4** and **7**).

The *cuica* is an instrument unique to Brazil. Its howling whine is produced by rubbing a wet cloth on a thin wooden rod attached to the skin of the drum. By pressing and stretching the skin with the fingers of the other hand, it is possible to vary the pitch (CD track **9**, 5:20–6:00).

From the largest *surdo,* almost the height of a man, to the rattling *tamborim,* all obey the signals from the very smallest of instruments, the *apito* (whistle) of the *bateria's mestre* (director).

Tamborim

CD track **9**, 6:15–6:26

Repique

CD track **14**, 1:00–1:25

Surdo   CD track **9**, 7:30–8:34

CD track **9**, 7:14–7:27

Reco-reco

Cuica   CD track **9**, 5:20–6:00

Agogô

Pratos

CD track **2**, 4:31–4:38

Tan-tan

Surdo   CD track **9**, 7:30–8:34

Pandeiro   CD track **7**, 1:14–1:34

Baianas

SEVENTY WOMEN DANCERS OVER FORTY-FIVE

A traditional element of the school's presentation, and one required in competition, is the group *(ala)* of *baianas,* made up of at least 70 women over the age of 45. Their costumes do not necessarily have to relate to the year's chosen theme, but full skirts, at least, are a must. Their costume is typical of Bahia, a state in the northeast of Brazil. Their elaborate gowns, created at the samba school's expense, weigh as much as 33 pounds (15 kilograms). Through most of the parade the *baianas* generally perform only a kind of rocking step to the rhythm of the samba, but on certain refrains they all spin like children's tops.

Mestre-sala and Porta-bandeira

THE PRIDE OF THE *ESCOLA*

The most important individuals in the parade are the *mestre-sala,* or master of ceremonies, and the *porta-bandeira,* or standard bearer.

They do not dance the samba; their movements are more like ballet. The master of ceremonies pays court to the standard bearer with stylized gestures and serves as her protector. The *porta-bandeira* is required to swing the school's colors with elegance and charm. Generally the best spot in the march is reserved for this couple, directly in front of the *bateria,* which inspires them to peak performance with its electrifying rhythm. The standard bearer's rapid pirouettes are carefully choreographed to correspond to dance interludes performed by the master of ceremonies.

Becoming a school's *porta-bandeira* is the highest honor a woman can attain in Carnival. Her dress and the costume of the *mestre-sala* are among the most expensive and elaborate of the entire *escola*. Naturally it is the samba school that foots the bill for them, for few performers could afford the costumes themselves. The samba school's director expects them to dance with perfection. A poor performance on the part of this crucial couple can botch a school's chance of winning. The strict rules of the competition allow judges to deduct points if parts of costume become detached and fall to the ground during the performance.

Comissão de frente

PRELUDE IN COSTUME AND DANCE

*I*n early Carnivals, the directors of the samba schools walked at the head of the parade greeting the spectators themselves. Today the *comissão de frente*, the greeting (or front) committee, is generally composed of no more than 15 tall men. Their costumes and movements introduce the school's chosen theme. In a distinct break with tradition, more and more women are finding spots in these important roles.

Since the first impression is all-important, *carnavalescos* strive to overwhelm the jurors and spectators with the splendor of the *comissão de frente*. A bit of unusual choreography or a surprising piece of theater on the part of the greeting committee can set the tone for a school's entire presentation.

The Competition

FORTY JURORS
CHOOSE THE WINNER

The *Desfile de Escolas de Samba do Grupo Especial* is a competition. This fantastic, playful test of strength fans the competitive spirit of all its participants and assistants.

From year to year, the concepts become increasingly successful and more original, the achievements greater. Along with the Brazilians' musicality and enthusiasm, it is the competitive aspect that has made Rio's Carnival the greatest event of its kind.

Each *escola* is loudly cheered by its fans during its parade (CD track **14**, 3:47–4:10), as it tries to win the victory and become champion *(campeã)* in its group, which is made up of from 10 to 14 schools. The top group, the Grupo Especial, with such well-known representatives as Mangueira, Portela, and Imperatriz, is followed in rank by Grupo A. Each group parades in the Sambódromo on a different day. The winners of the first two places in Group A take part in the Grupo Especial's parade in the following year, while the bottom two from the Grupo Especial fall back into Grupo A. Those schools that fail to maintain their position in this group are relegated to Grupo B, which holds its parades in the city center on the Avenida Rio Branco-—before an equally vast and enthusiastic public, but far from the television cameras.

Forty jurors judge the school's presentation on the basis of ten criteria: *enredo* (theme), *samba enredo* (presentation of the theme in song), *harmonia* (harmony in song and rhythm), *evolução* (commitment and enthusiasm of the participants), *conjunto* (impression made by the entire school), *alegorias é adereços* (allegorical floats), *fantasias* (costumes), *comissão de frente* (greeting committee), *mestre-sala é porta-bandeira* (master of ceremonies and standard bearer), and *bateria* (rhythm band).

Ash Wednesday draws the people of Rio to their television sets like a soccer playoff game. In a live broadcast, each juror's rating for the various criteria is read off. A *nota deiz* (highest score ten) elicits cheers from the fans of the given school. A nine is already cause for disappointment, and an eight—even from only a single juror—dashes any hope of victory. With the announcement of even lower scores, viewers are quick to suspect that the jurors were bribed. After more than an hour, it is clear which school came out on top, and thousands of fans stream to its clubhouse *(quadra)* to celebrate. The results serve as a topic of conversation for weeks, and give the press ample material for in-depth commentary.

PARADE WINNERS 1967-1999

1967	Mangueira	1978	Beja Flor	1989	Imperatriz
1968	Mangueira	1979	Mocidade	1990	Mocidade
1969	Salgueiro	1980	Beja Flor, Portela, Imperatriz	1991	Mocidade
1970	Portela	1981	Imperatriz	1992	Estácio de Sá
1971	Salgueiro	1982	Império Serrano	1993	Salgueiro
1972	Império Serrano	1983	Beja Flor	1994	Imperatriz
1973	Mangueira	1984	Mangueira	1995	Imperatriz
1974	Salgueiro	1985	Mocidade	1996	Mocidade
1975	Salgueiro	1986	Mangueira	1997	Viradouro
1976	Beja Flor	1987	Mangueira	1998	Mangueira and Beja Flor
1977	Beja Flor	1988	Vila Isabel	1999	Imperatriz

Preparation

THOUSANDS WORKING IN SECRET

Work on the costumes and allegorical floats continues right up until the day of the parade, with an amazing attention to detail. Thousands of seamstresses, most of them working at home, as well as mechanics, coach builders, carpenters, electricians, and sculptors earn their living on commission from the samba schools.

Preparations for the event take a year. They are undertaken in the greatest secrecy, for it would be disastrous if the surprises in store for the spectators and the jury were known to other samba schools in advance. The schools' workshops are carefully guarded, and only those above all suspicion are admitted.

The Grand Parade

AMAZEMENT IS THE KEY

The parade participants, the samba school's organizers and directors, the spectators, the reporters from around the world—everyone feels the anticipation.

For the dancers, singers, and musicians, the procession is the fulfillment of a dream, one that has made their difficult lives more bearable for a year. At Carnival time, social distinctions that make life so hard for so many no longer apply. The industrialist masquerades as a clown, the dock worker as King Solomon, the housemaid as a celebrated samba star of the Sambódromo, the government minister as a *surdo* player and the taxi driver as his *mestre de bateria*, the jobless girl from the *favela* as a ravishing Cleopatra—all come together in the rhythm of the samba and a desire to emerge victorious. For all of them, the parade is 80 minutes of excitement and intoxicating color-—and for many pain, frustration, and failure. Eighty minutes of another, more rapturous life leaving them happy and exhausted.

Cameramen from around the world try to capture the color and variety of the all-too-evanescent Carnival. Spectators succumb to the pure joy of rediscovering something they thought they had lost with their childhood: the capacity for sheer enchantment.

Sambódromo

WHERE FANTASY REIGNS

he days of the grand parades bring color to Rio's cityscape. Ordinary bus and subway stations are suddenly alive with glamour, glitter, and lavish costumes. In anticipation of their performance, many of the samba schools' participants and fans begin singing their Carnival songs on the platforms. In this holiday mood thousands of people are united by a single goal.

Since 1984, the parade of the top samba schools takes place in a stadium of its own, the Sambódromo, on Rua Marquês de Sapucaí. It was designed by the famous Brazilian architect Oscar Niemeyer. The rest of the year it teems with school-children, its loges serving as classrooms. The *passarela do samba,* or samba concourse, is 590 yards (540 meters) long and 42.5 feet (13 meters) wide.

Each night of Carnival some 35,000 marchers, musicians, and dancers stream into the samba stadium, where they are awaited by 60,000 spectators.

Each samba school has precisely 80 minutes for its presentation. If it goes beyond its time limit or if its timing misfires, either because a float runs into trouble or its various elements fall apart, it is penalized by the judges. The *escolas* begin their parades at an assembly ground called the Concentração and finally disperse at the Praça da Apoteose, beneath the Sambódromo's symbol, a gigantic concrete arch.

Concentração

THE FOCUS OF ALL HOPES

*J*ust outside the Sambódromo lies the Concentração, where the parade participants prepare for their performance. After a year of preparation, the anticipation of the samba school's performers, as many as 5,000 people, is enormous.

Costumes, carefully transported through the city, are put on, adjusted, and if necessary given a few last-minute stitches.

The school's organizers arrange the various groups of dancers *(alas)* in the proper sequence and make sure that the floats are ready to go.

In the final moments before the start, the sense of expectation on the part of both the spectators and the participants is fanned by the loud entrance of the school's *bateria* and singers (CD tracks **2, 4, 7, 12, 17, 19**).

Carros alegóricos

MOVING PALACES

The samba school's chosen theme is visibly reflected in its *carros alegóricos* (allegorical floats). Each school is expected to produce five to eight of these palaces on wheels. They must be no more than 28 feet (8.5 meters) wide and 33 feet (10 meters) tall. Each of them weighs several tons, and it takes as many as 30 men to push them.

At the Concentração, giant cranes lift the dancers onto the higher parts of the floats, where they will courageously perform in heavy and unwieldy costumes on shaky platforms as little as three feet wide and 25 feet above the ground. The *carnavalescos* pour all of their imagination and creativity into the design of these floats. Light orgies, waterfalls and pools, giant theaters and classical palaces, animal sculptures, ships, and trains—each seems more marvelous than the last.

The men who push the floats are a special fraternity, and many boast of having performed this heavy task for years. Motorized floats are not allowed, so the huge contraptions, often weighing as much as five tons, must be propelled with sheer muscle power. What makes it especially difficult is the need to brake suddenly to allow the dancers to perform. The men pushing the float generally cannot see what is happening, so they must be guided by a special pilot, who at times urges them on like a virtual slavedriver. If a float falls behind because of poor coordination or if it bumps into the fence, often a mere three feet away, the school's presentation is disrupted and its chances of winning are destroyed.

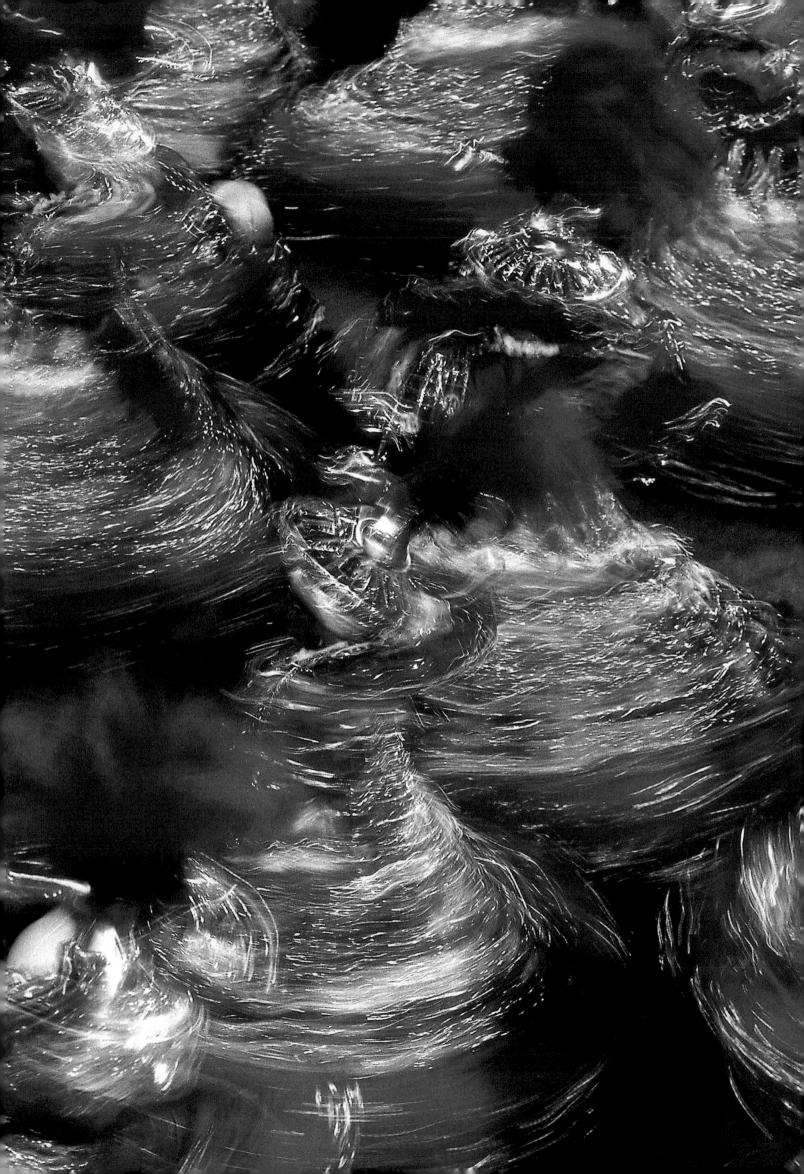

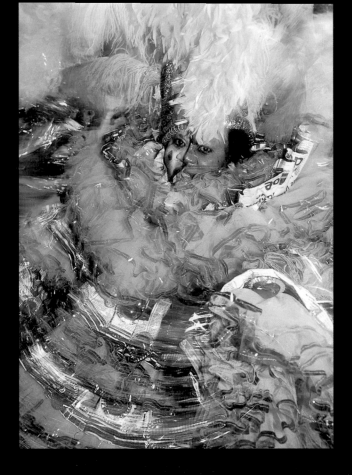

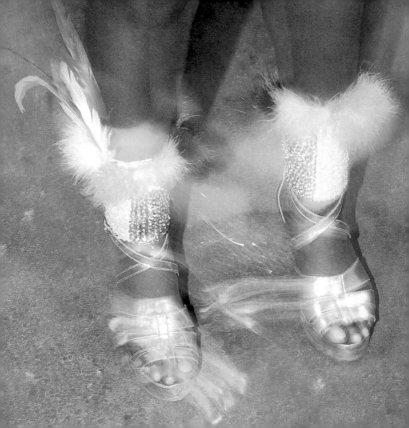

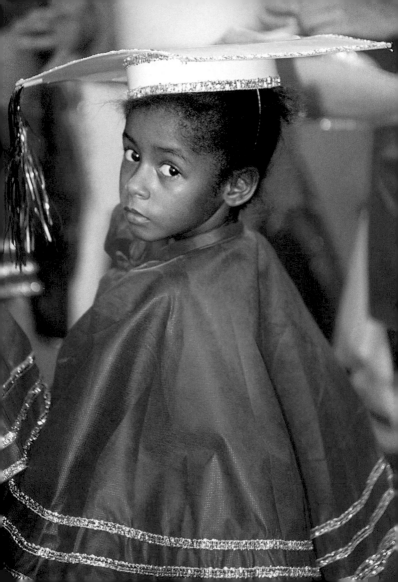

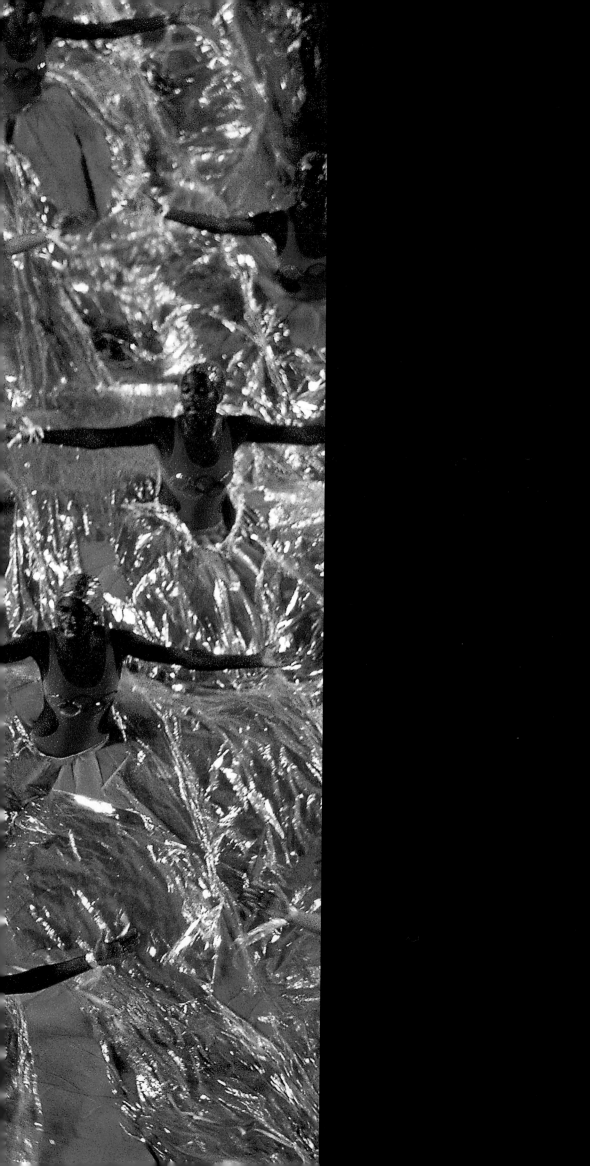

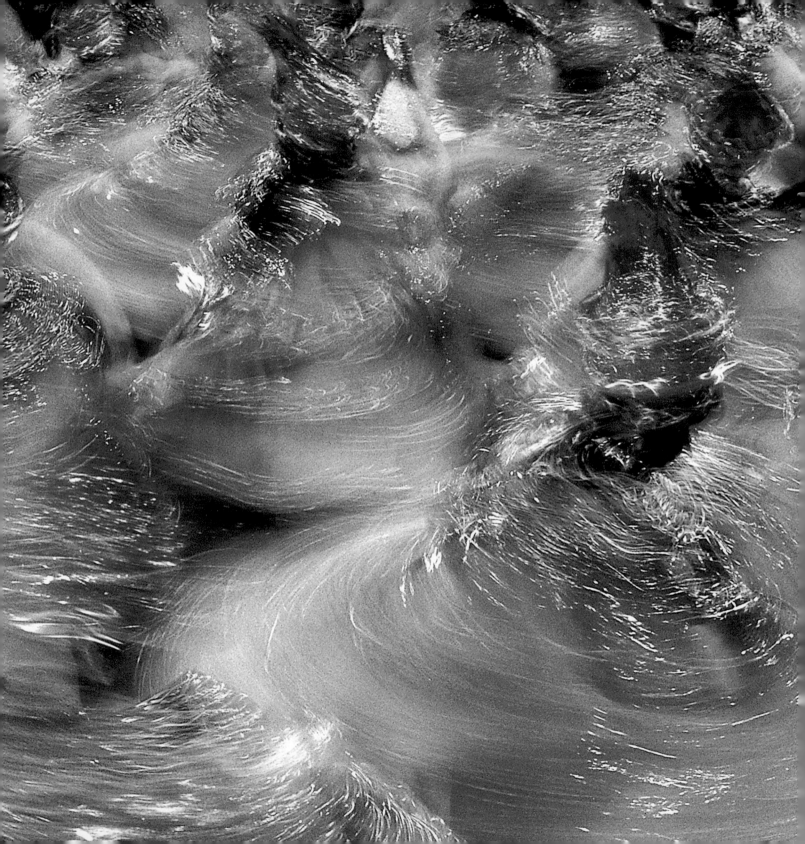

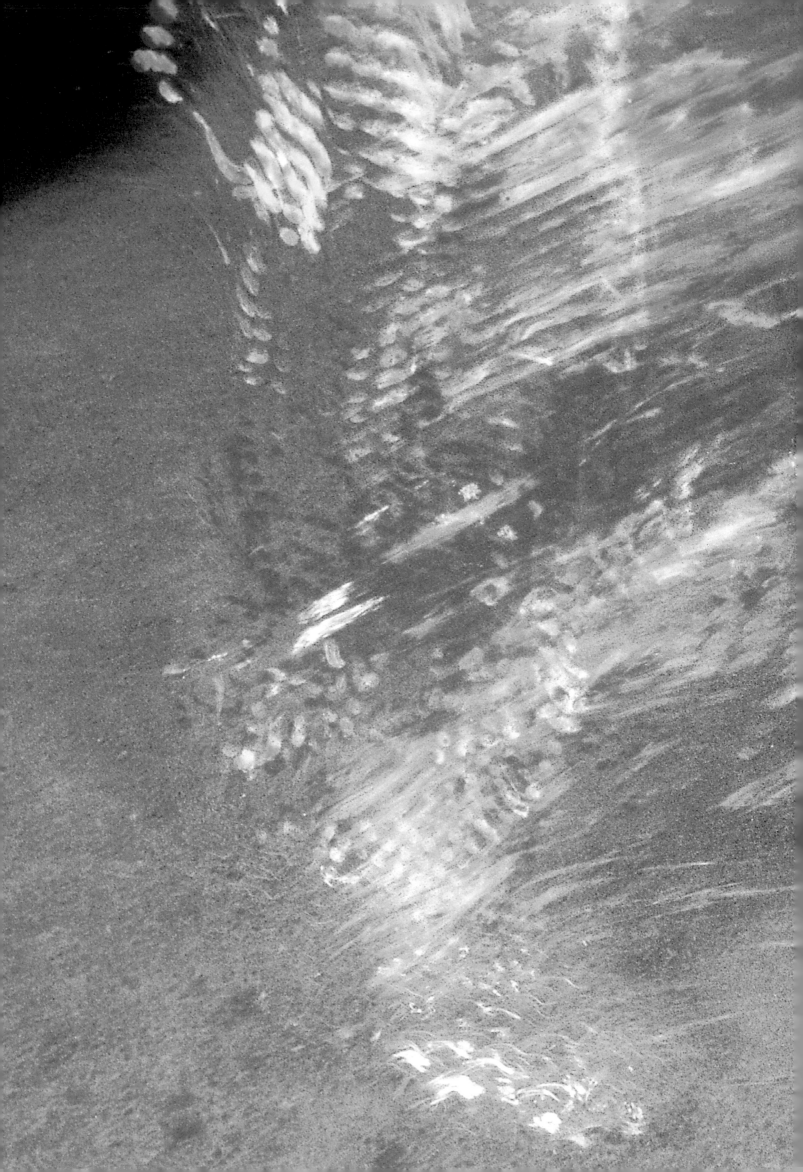

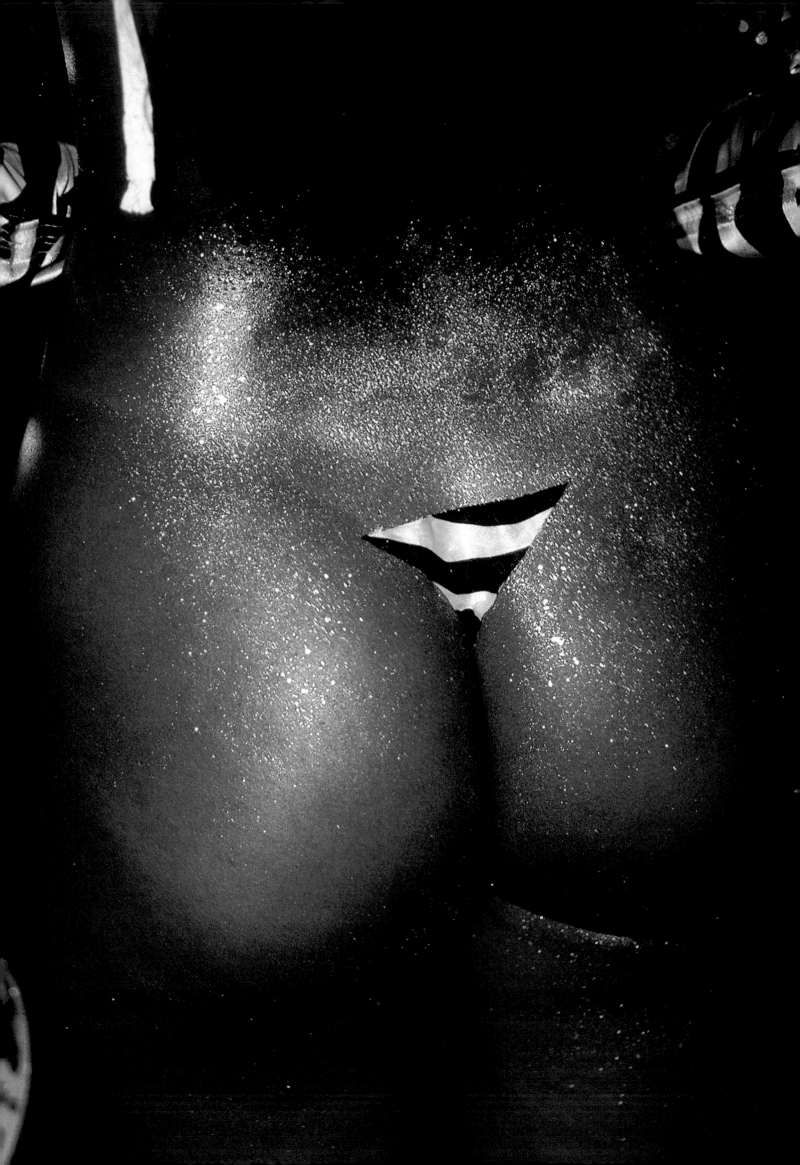

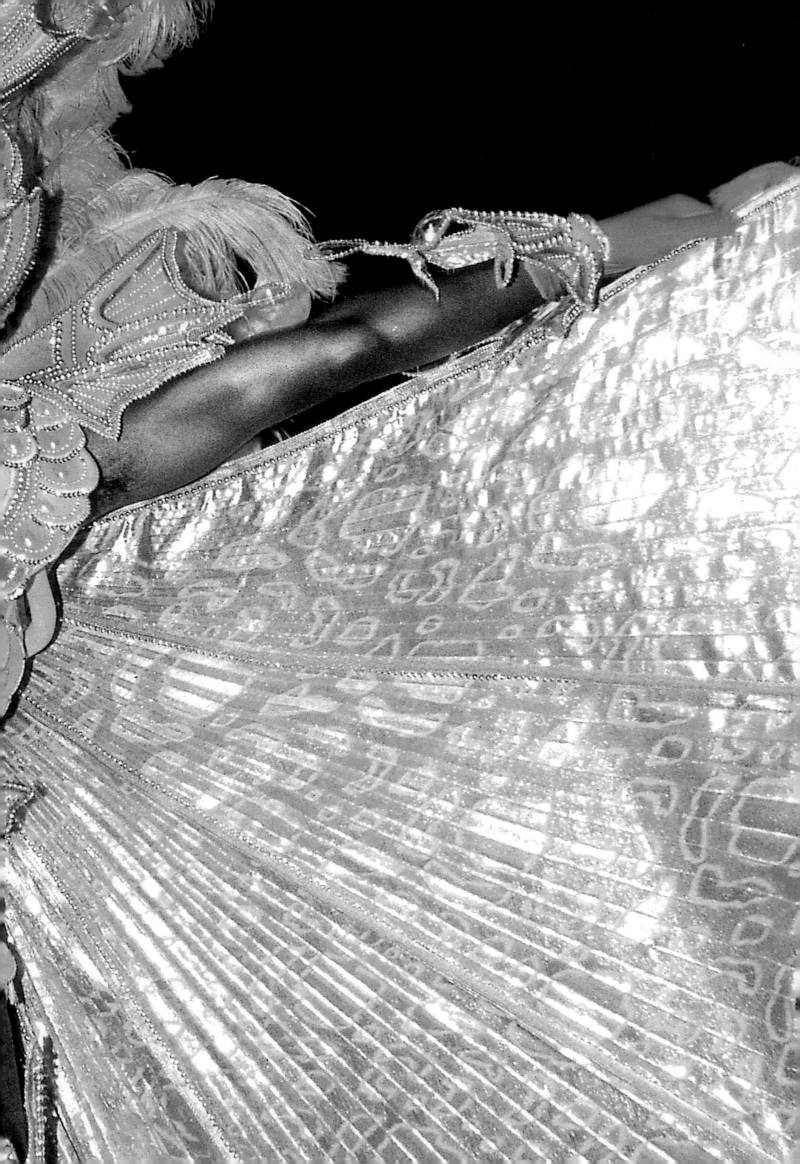

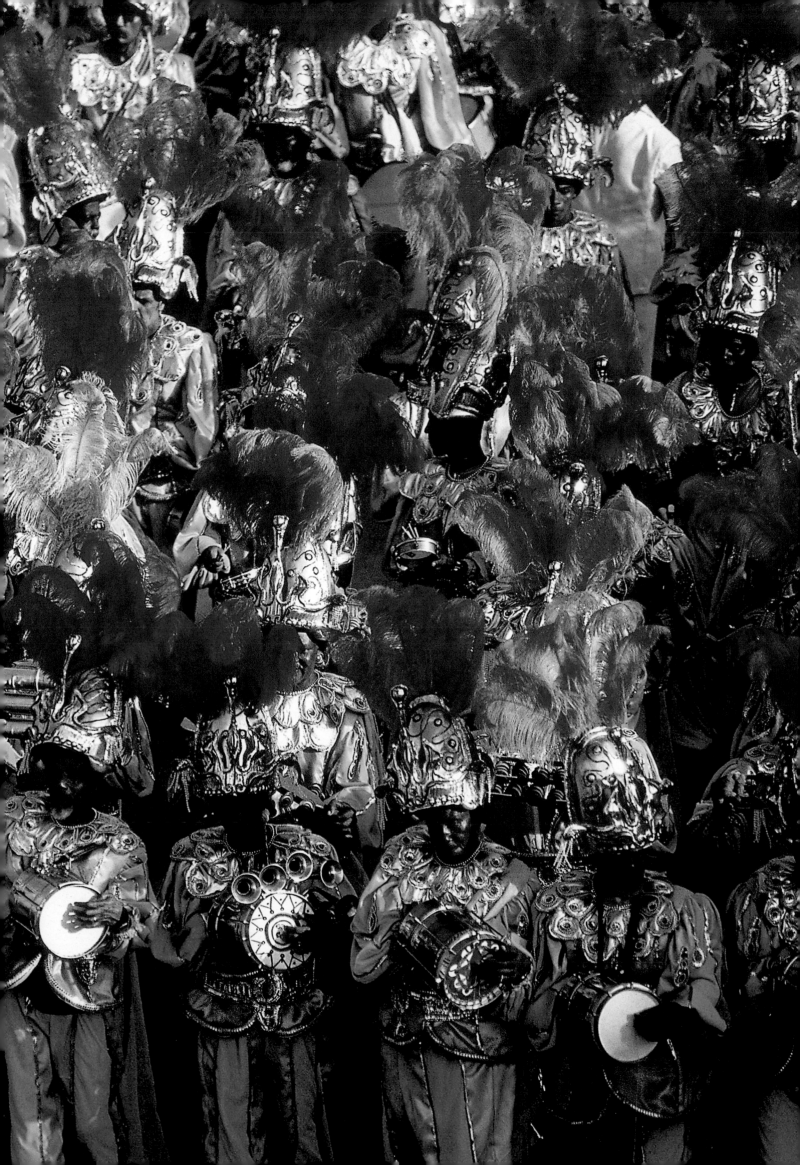

The Sadness of Dreams Fulfilled

The colors have dispersed, the rhythm has stopped, the crown has been set aside. Only a moment ago, while the *surdo* banished all thought of tomorrow, the Queen of Sheba danced, the sun and moon shone, and a star illuminated the shadows.

Gray reality awaits at the parade's end. But it cannot touch those who are already nursing that small ray of light, the dream of next year's Carnival.

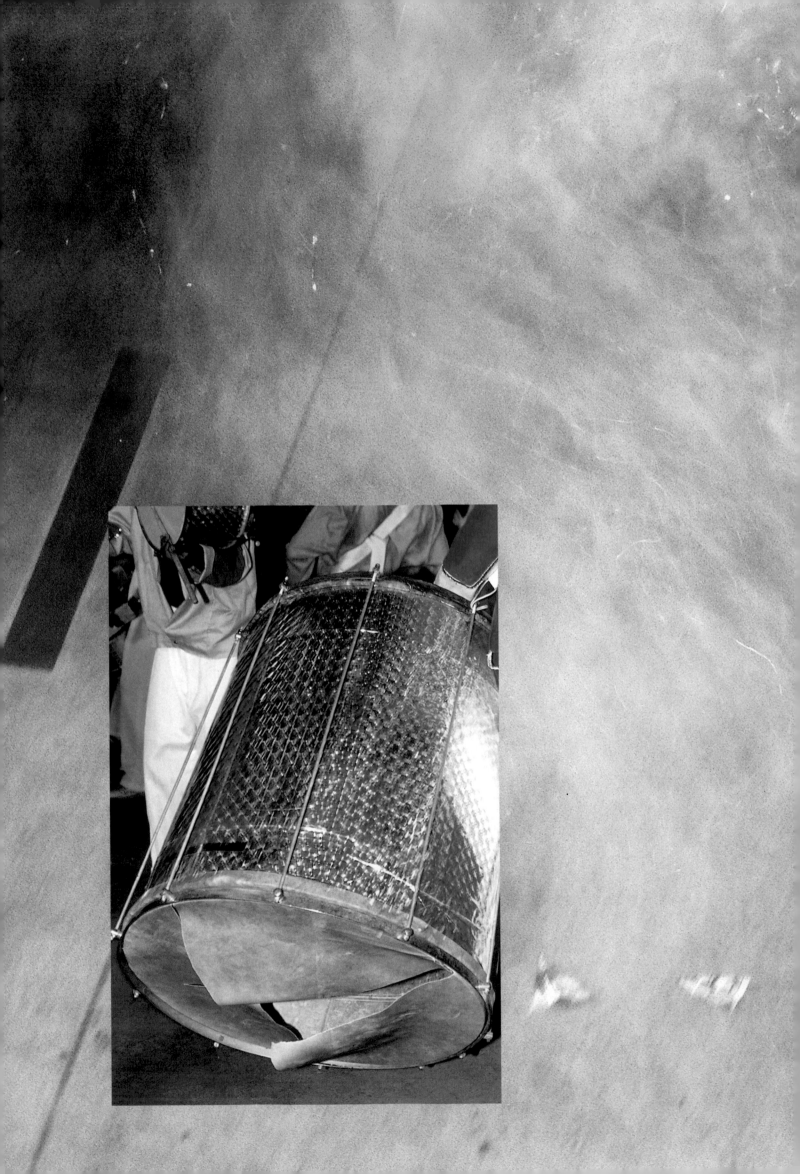

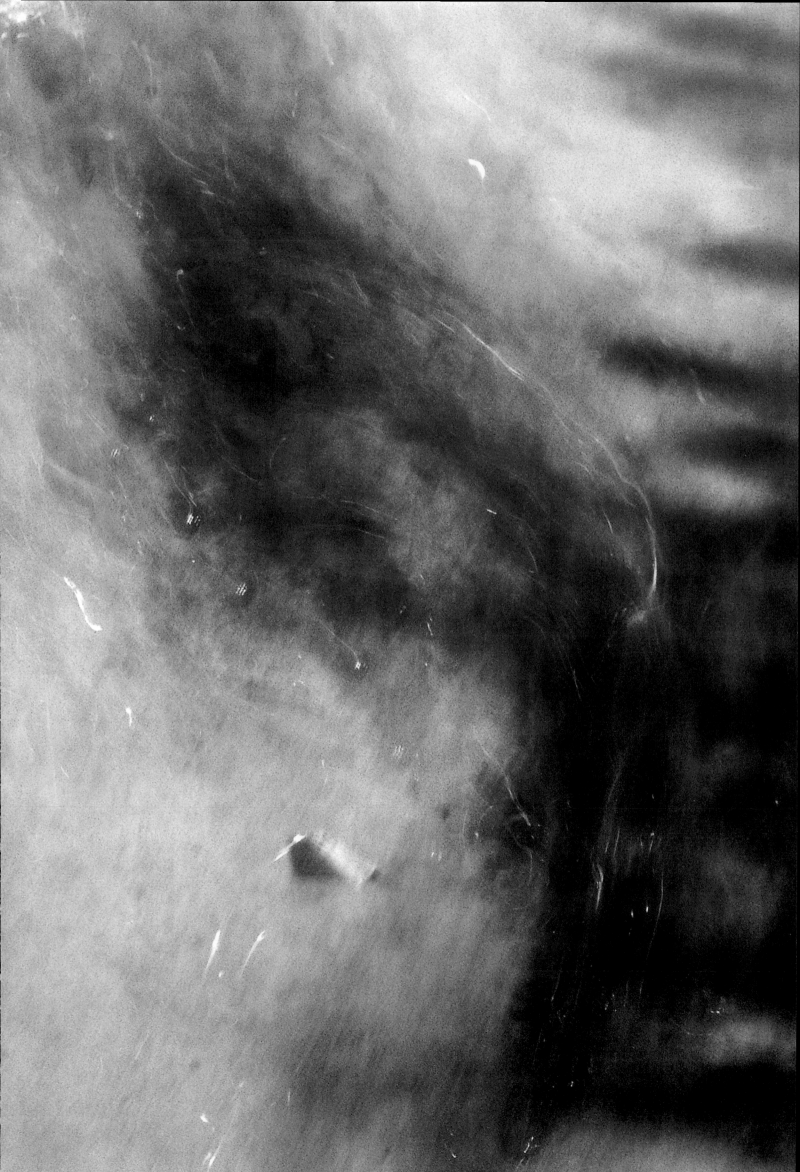

DETAILS OF THE LIVE RECORDINGS

1. *Pagode:* samba beneath the trees each Sunday. Everyone joins in singing.
2. The *bateria* of the samba school União da Ilha and the spectators inspire each other. In dialogue with other instruments, a *repique* in the background introduces the playing of the rhythm band, more than 300 strong.
4. Manguiera's *bateria* turns into the stadium from the Concentração, at first playing only its *cuicas*. Then the entire band takes up the school's characteristic rhythm with the accent on the second beat.
6. The Império Serrano *bateria* opens its performance with its *agogôs* (cowbells).
7. For more than three decades, Jamelão has been the lead singer for Manguiera. He opens the parade with the school's hymn, then the *bateria* begins to play.
9. As the spectators cheer *"É campeã!"* (it's the champion), the Imperatriz Leopoldinense *bateria* begins to play. In the second half of this longer, highly rhythmic recording, you can hear the sounds of the different instruments.
10. The Carnival song of the Salgueiro samba school, sung by its 5,000 performers.
12. The samba school Arranco, from Grupo A, the challengers to the Grupo Especial, takes up its song at the Concentração in 1998.
14. The Mocidade *bateria* opens with its typical rattling sound in 1999.
15. After 34 seconds the 1997 Mocidade song, sung by all of the samba school's dancers, segues into studio recording No. 16.
17. After 2:18 minutes the Manguiera song as sung by Jamelão and Eraldo Caê at its 1998 parade segues into studio recording No. 18.
19. Performers of the samba school Tradição strike up their song at the Concentração.

Additional Literature on Brazilian Music:
The Brazilian Sound—Samba, Bossa Nova, and the Popular Music of Brazil, by Chris McGowan and Ricardo Pessanha, Billboard Books—Watson Guptill Publications, New York, 1991.

CONTENTS OF THE CD

Compilation (P) and © 1999
by Helmut Teissl, Villach, Austria

Mastered by Tonstudio Weikert,
Feldkirchen, Austria
TW 992975

1. Live: *Pagode,* © Helmut Teissl   1:58

2. Live: *Bateria* of the *escola* União da Ilha at its appearance in 1996, © Helmut Teissl   4:41

3. Sambas de Enredo das Escolas de Samba do Grupo Especial 1994: G.R.E.S. União da Ilha do Governador "Abrakadabra, o despertar dos Mágicos," Quinho   4:15
(P) 1993 Gravadora Escola de Samba Ltda.
Courtesy of BMG Brazil Ltda.

4. Live: *Bateria* of the *escola* Estação Primeira de Manguiera begins its parade in 1998, © Helmut Teissl   1:19

5. Sambas de Enredo das Escolas de Samba do Grupo Especial Carnaval 1995: G.R.E.S. Estação Oruneura de Nabgyeura "A esmeralda do atlântico," Jamelão   3:37
(P) 1994 Gravadora Escola de Samba Ltda.
Courtesy of BMG Brazil Ltda.

6. Live: *Bateria* of the *escola* Império Serrano with its *agogôs* 1998, © Helmut Teissl   4:22

7. Live: Estação Primeira de Manguiera. Jamelão with "Exaltação á Mangueira" at the Concentração before the 1996 parade, © Helmut Teissl   2:16

8. Sambas de Enredo das Escolas de Samba do Grupo Especial 1990: G.R.E.S. Estação Primeira de Manguiera "E Deu a louca no barroco," Jamelão   4:21
(P) 1989 Gravadoa Escola de Samba Ltda.
Courtesy of BMG Brazil Ltda.

9. Live: *Bateria* of the *escola* Imperatriz Leopoldinense at the start of its 1999 parade and individual instruments of a *bateria,* © Helmut Teissl   9:01

10. Live: *Escola* Acadêmicos do Salgueiro in its 1994 parade, © Helmut Teissl   1:00

11. Sambas de Enredo das Escolas de Samba do Grupo Especial Carnaval 1994: G.R.E.S. Acadêmicos do Salgueiro "Rio de Lá pra Cá," Quinzinho   3:53
(P) 1993 Gravadora Escola de Samba Ltda.
Courtesy of BMG Brazil Ltda.

12. Live: *Escola* Arranco at the Concentração at the start of its parade in 1998, © Helmut Teissl   2:53

13. Sambas de Enredo das Escolas de Samba do Grupo Especial Carnaval 1994: G.R.E.S. Estação Primeira de Manguiera "Atrás da verde-e-rosa só não vai quem já morreu," Jamelão   4:08
(P) 1993 Gravadora Escola de Samba Ltda.
Courtesy of BMG Brazil Ltda.

14. Live: *Bateria* of the *escola* Mocidade Independente de Padre Miguel starts to play in 1996, © Helmut Teissl   5:07

15. Live: The entire *escola* Mocidade at its parade in 1997, © Helmut Teissl   0:34

16. Sambas de Enredo das Escolas de Samba do Grupo Especial Carnaval 1997: G.R.E.S. Mocidade Independente de Padre Miguel "De corpo e alma na avenida," Wander Pires   2:38
(P) 1996 Gravadora Escola de Samba Ltda.
Courtesy of BMG Brazil Ltda.

17. Live: Sambas de Enredo Grupo Especial ao vivo na Sapucai 1998: G.R.E.S. Estação Primeira de Manguiera "Chico Buarque da Mangueira," Jamelão and Eraldo Caê   2:18
(P) 1998 Gravadora Escola de Samba Ltda.
Courtesy of BMG Brazil Ltda.

18. Sambas de Enredo das Escolas de Samba do Grupo Especial 1998: G.R.E.S. Estação Primeira de Manguiera "Chico Buarque da Mangueira," Jamelão and Eraldo Caê   2:38
(P) 1997 Gravadora Escola de Samba Ltda.
Courtesy of BMG Brazil Ltda.

19. Live: *Esquenta na Sapucai:* G.R.E.S. Tradição opening song 1998, "Tô dentro, tô fora," Taroba   5:34
(P) 1998 Escola de Samba (BMG).
Courtesy of BMG Brazil Ltda.

20. Sambas de Enredo das Escolas de Samba do Grupo Especial 1997: G.R.E.S. União da Ilha do Governador "Cidade maravilhosa, o sonho de pereira passos," Ito Melodia   5:25
(P) 1996 Gravadora Escola de Samba Ltda.
Courtesy of BMG Brazil Ltda.

Total running time: 72:10

ACKNOWLEDGMENTS

I am indebted to a number of optimistic and helpful people for helping me get the book *Carnival in Rio* into print:

Most of all to Walter Primosch and the Kärnten *Tageszeitung* for their support over the years, to Christine Laut, Vienna, for her initial enthusiasm for the pictures and many suggestions at the undertaking of the book project, to Christian Brandstätter for his interest in publishing the book, to Karin Schuhmann of BMG Munich for graciously initiating me into the legal intricacies of music publishing, to Marcelo Falcão, Fernando Camargo, and Ana Maria de Sá Pereira of BMG Brasil Ltda, Rio de Janeiro, for obtaining all the use rights for the CD that accompanies the book, Sr. Zacarias de Siqueira de Oliveira of the Gravadora de Samba Ltda, Rio de Janeiro, for permitting me to use my live recordings in the Sambódromo, to Peter Weikert for his dedication in the preparation of the CD.

Special thanks are owed to Maria-Inés Gomide, Rio de Janeiro, for contacts with the samba schools and musicians and for her valuable corrections of the book's content and her sympathy during the ups and downs in the creation of the book.

Many of my friends at home helped me in the difficult selection of pictures.

But it is to my family that I owe the greatest thanks, to my wife Reini and my daughters Karin and Christine for their patience and forbearance in sacrificing many evenings to my creative work.

Finally, I am deeply grateful to the people of Rio de Janeiro for their friendliness, openness, humanity, and their ability to communicate their love of life especially in the turbulent Carnival period. I am wholly in awe of their creativity and musicality and full of admiration for them.

Helmut Teissl

Text and Photographs: Helmut Teissl
Translator: Russell Stockman
Editor: Richard Koss
Designer: Patricia Fabricant
Production Director: Louise Kurtz

First published in the United States of America in 2000 by Abbeville Publishing Group
22 Cortlandt Street, New York, NY 10007

First published in 1999 by Verlag Christian Brandstätter, A-1010 Vienna, Schwarzenbergstrasse 5, Austria

Text copyright c 1999 Verlag Christian Brandstätter, Vienna

First Edition
10 9 8 7 6 5 4 3 2 1

Library of Congress Cataloging-in-Publication Data available upon request

ISBN: 0-7892-0642-0
Printed in Italy